My Bible Study Notebook

This notebook was designed and illustrated by Eunice Wilkie
Copyright © 2019

Scripture quotations have been taken from The Holy Bible, New King James Version®.
© 1982 by Thomas Nelson, Inc. Used by permission. All rights reserved.

THIS NOTEBOOK BELONGS TO:

DATE & CONTACT DETAILS:

MY FAVOURITE HYMN OR SONG:

MY FAVOURITE BIBLE VERSE:

OTHER THINGS I LOVE ABOUT THE BIBLE:

In the beginning God created the heavens and the earth.
(Genesis 1:1)

Did you know...?
The first word in the Bible is *'In'*
The last word in the Bible is *'Amen'*

*For God so loved the world that He gave His only begotten Son,
that whoever believes in Him should not perish
but have everlasting life.* (John 3:16)

Did you know…?
The longest word in the Bible is: Mahershalalhashbaz

The LORD is longsuffering and abundant in mercy.
(Numbers 14:18)

Did you know...?
There are 66 books in the Bible:
39 books in the Old Testament, 27 books in the New Testament

You shall love the LORD your God with all your heart, with all your soul, and with all your strength.
(Deuteronomy 6:5)

Did you know...?
There are 31,101 verses in the Bible

Choose for yourselves this day whom you will serve.
(Joshua 24:15)

Did you know…?
The shortest book in the New Testament is 3 John

As for me and my house, we will serve the LORD.
(Joshua 24:15)

Did you know...?
40 different writers wrote the Bible - all inspired by God

I will praise You, for I am fearfully and wonderfully made; marvellous are Your works, and that my soul knows very well.
(Psalm 139:14)

Did you know...?
The longest book in the Old Testament is the book of Psalms

*I will lift up my eyes to the hills - from whence comes my help?
My help comes from the LORD, Who made heaven and earth.*
(Psalm 121:1-2)

Did you know...?
The Bible has been ranslated into more than 1,200 languages

*Trust in the LORD with all your heart,
and lean not on your own understanding.*
(Proverbs 3:5)

Did you know...?
The longest verse in the Bible is Esther 8:9

*In all your ways acknowledge Him (God),
and He shall direct your paths.*
(Proverbs 3:6)

Did you know...?
The shortest verse in the Bible is John 11:35: *Jesus wept*

Remember now your Creator in the days of your youth.
(Ecclesiastes 12:1)

Did you know...?
The shortest book in the Old Testament is Obadiah

All we like sheep have gone astray; we have turned, every one, to his own way; and the LORD has laid on Him the iniquity of us all.
(Isaiah 53:6)

Did you know...?
There are 1,189 chapters in the Bible

Through the LORD'S mercies we are not consumed, because His compassions fail not. They are new every morning;. great is Your faithfulness. (Lamentations 3:22-23)

Did you know...?
There are approximately 1,260 promises in the Bible

Whoever calls on the name of the LORD shall be saved.
(Joel 2:32)

Did you know...?
There are more than 8,000 predictions / prophecies in the Bible

*What does the LORD require of you but to do justly, to love mercy,
and to walk humbly with your God.*
(Micah 6:8)

Did you know…?
There are approximately 3,268 verses about fulfilled prophecy in the Bible

The LORD is good, a stronghold in the day of trouble;
and He knows those who trust in Him.
(Nahum 1:7)

Did you know...?
There are 3,294 questions in the Bible

The LORD your God in your midst, the Mighty One, will save; He will rejoice over you with gladness, He will quiet you with His love, He will rejoice over you with singing. (Zephaniah 3:17)

Did you know…?
The longest book in the New Testament is the gospel of Luke

Did you know...?
The shortest chapter in the Bible is Psalm 117

Ask, and it will be given to you; seek, and you will find; knock, and it will be opened to you.
(Matthew 7:7)

Did you know…?
There are approximately 3,566,480 letters in an English Bible

But He was wounded for our transgressions, He was bruised for our iniquities; the chastisement for our peace was upon Him, and by His stripes we are healed. (Isaiah 53:5)

Did you know...?
The shortest verse in the Old Testament is 1 Chronicles 1:25

Follow Me, and I will make you become fishers of men.
(Mark 1:17)

Did you know…?
There are five different types of books in the Old Testament:
Law; History; Wisdom & Poetry; Major Prophets; Minor Prophets.

For where your treasure is, there your heart will be also.
(Luke 12:34)

Did you know...?
There are five different types of books in the New Testament:
Gospels; History; Paul's Epistles; General Epistles; Prophecy.

For God did not send His Son into the world to condemn the world, but that the world through Him might be saved.
(John 3:17)

Did you know…?
The longest non-name words in the Old Testament are:
evilfavouredness and lovingkindness

Nor is there salvation in any other, for there is no other name under heaven given among men by which we must be saved.
(Acts 4:12)

Did you know...?
The midpoint books in the Bible are Micah and Nahum

Surely He has borne our griefs and carried our sorrows.
(Isaiah 53:4)

Did you know…?
There are approximately 6,468 commands in the Bible

We know that all things work together for good to those who love God, to those who are the called according to His purpose.
(Romans 8:28)

Did you know...?
Over 100 million copies of the Bible are sold each year

*And now abide faith, hope, love, these three;
but the greatest of these is love.*
(1 Corinthians 13:13)

Did you know...?
Events in the Bible primarily take place across three continents:
Asia, Africa, and Europe

The Son of Man has come to seek and to save that which was lost.
(Luke 19:10)

Did you know...?
The Bible is the best-selling book in history, with total sales exceeding 5 billion copies

*For He made Him who knew no sin to be sin for us,
that we might become the righteousness of God in Him.*
(2 Corinthians 5:21)

Did you know...?
The books of the Old Testament were written before the birth of Christ; the New Testament covers the life of Christ and beyond

The fruit of the Spirit is love, joy, peace, longsuffering, kindness, goodness, faithfulness, gentleness, self-control.
(Galatians 5:22-23)

Did you know...?
The Bible was written in 3 languages: Hebrew, Aramaic, and Greek

Do not worry about tomorrow, for tomorrow will worry about its own things. Sufficient for the day is its own trouble.
(Matthew 6:34)

Did you know...?
There are about 185 songs in the Bible:
about 150 of these are in the Psalms

"The LORD is my portion," says my soul, "therefore I hope in Him!"
(Lamentations 3:24)

Did you know...?
There are 21 dreams recorded in the Bible

*For by grace you have been saved through faith,
and that not of yourselves; it is the gift of God, not of works,
lest anyone should boast.* (Ephesians 2:8-9)

Did you know...?
The Bible was written over a 1600 year period;
the time of writing was from approximately 1500 BC to AD 100

Be anxious for nothing, but in everything by prayer and supplication, with thanksgiving, let your requests be made known to God. (Philippians 4:6)

Did you know...?
Each of the books in the Bible, except 5, are divided into chapters and verses. The 5 which aren't divided by chapters are:
Obadiah, Philemon, 2 John, 3 John, and Jude

Believe on the Lord Jesus Christ, and you will be saved.
(Acts 16:31)

Did you know…?
The middle chapter of the Bible is Psalm 117

Do not grow weary in doing good.
(2 Thessalonians 3:13)

Did you know...?
The Old Testament was originally written in Hebrew, whereas the New Testament was written in Greek

Christ Jesus came into the world to save sinners.
(1 Timothy 1:15)

Did you know...?
Ezra 7:21 contains every letter of the English alphabet apart from the letter 'j'

*Not by works of righteousness which we have done,
but according to His mercy He saved us.*
(Titus 3:5)

Did you know...?
The oldest man ever in the history of mankind
was 'Methuselah' who lived for 969 years

Let us run with endurance the race that is set before us, looking unto Jesus, the author and finisher of our faith.
(Hebrews 12:1-2)

Did you know…?
The phrase 'do not be afraid' can be found 365 times in the Bible
(the same as the number of days in a year)

*I am the good shepherd.
The good shepherd gives His life for the sheep.*
(John 10:11)

Did you know...?
Enoch and Elijah were the only two people who never died; instead they were directly taken up to heaven by God

Jesus said to him, "I am the way, the truth, and the life. No one comes to the Father except through Me."
(John 14:6)

Did you know...?
The Bible was the first book to be printed, in approximately 1455

If we confess our sins, He is faithful and just to forgive us our sins and to cleanse us from all unrighteousness.
(1 John 1:9)

Did you know...?
Samson was the strongest man in the Bible,
whereas Solomon was the wisest

Let your gentleness be known to all men. The Lord is at hand.
(Philippians 4:5)

Did you know...?
When Noah built the ark, he was already 600 years old,
and he died when he was 950 years old

Rejoice in the Lord always.
(Philippians 4:4)

Did you know...?
The most commonly used person's name in the Bible is *David*;
it occurs approximately 1,139 times

*The Lord ... is not willing that any should perish
but that all should come to repentance.*
(2 Peter 3:9)

Did you know...?
The most commonly used place name in the Bible is *Israel*;
it occurs approximately 2,575 times

Whatever things are true, whatever things are noble, whatever things are just, whatever things are pure, whatever things are lovely .... meditate on these things. (Philippians 4:8)

Did you know...?
1 Chronicles 4:10 contains every letter of the English alphabet, apart from the letter 'z'

Casting all your care upon Him, for He cares for you.
(1 Peter 5:7)

Did you know…?
There are 19 names in the Bible which are the same
for men and women, e.g. Noah (1 man, 1 woman)

In this is love, not that we loved God, but that He loved us and sent His Son to be the propitiation for our sins.
(1 John 4:10)

Did you know...?
9 people in the Bible had their names changed,
e.g. Abram to Abraham, Jacob to Israel

To God our Saviour, Who alone is wise, be glory and majesty, dominion and power, both now and forever. Amen.
(Jude verse 25)

Worthy is the Lamb who was slain to receive power and riches and wisdom, and strength and honour and glory and blessing!
(Revelation 5:12)

Printed in Great Britain by Bell and Bain Ltd, Glasgow